The Art and Science of
HORSESHOEING

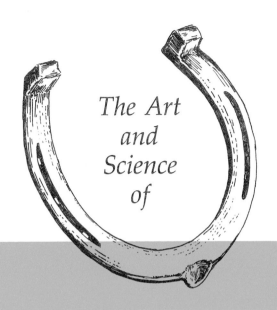

*The Art
and
Science
of*

HORSESHOEING

R. Gordon Greeley, B.S., M.S., D.V.M.

Drawings by the Author

J. B. LIPPINCOTT COMPANY
Philadelphia and Toronto

Library of Congress Catalog Card Number 72-134863

ISBN-0-397-50253-2

Printed in the United States of America

5   6   4

Dedicated to my wife
Dorothy
with love

Foreword

Through association with veterinary and other students the author has become aware of a desire on the part of many for an available source of information concerning the everyday, fundamental aspects of horseshoeing. During the postwar forties the author experienced the same desire and even adopted horseshoeing as a trade. As a life's work horseshoeing didn't seem too promising. At that time the popularity of the horse was just emerging from the doldrums, and so full-time application to the trade was abandoned in favor of veterinary studies. During subsequent years in practice and teaching the knowledge has been quite useful, and a lively interest in the subject has been maintained.

There are several excellent schools of horseshoeing in the United States, and in most areas the services of competent farriers are available. The finished farrier is a man of substantial accomplishment; this volume does not, in its limited scope, pretend to produce farriers. It is intended rather to add to the enjoyment of the horseman in his animals and to increase his self-reliance through knowledge, although the likelihood is excellent that a horseman who studies the text well and makes the necessary sacrifices in time and physical effort may find himself well on the way to becoming a competent craftsman of the art.

The greatest advances in horseshoeing, led by the veterinary colleges, occurred in the 18th and 19th centuries. The greatest impetus was the spur of military expedience. By the turn of the 20th century horseshoeing had crystallized into an art and a science. Texts written in that period are still among the best and are the bedrock for reference to this day. The author's favorite is *Handbook of Horseshoeing* by J. A. W. Dollar, published by W. R. Jenkins, London, 1898. Another good one is *Text-book of Horseshoeing* by A. Lungwitz and J. W. Adams, edition 11, published by J. B. Lippincott, Philadelphia, 1913. Both books have been long out of print and are likely to be found in the rare book section of a library that possesses them.

Besides the omissions in this text, some of the concepts may inspire controversy. Remember, horseshoeing is certainly an art and certainly a science, but not an exact science. There are too many exceptions to the rules. Many misconceptions linger from the last century, and it cannot be denied that some may turn up in this volume, for the author was trained by elderly farriers who harbored some misconceptions handed on to them in their apprenticeship in the early 20th century.

In the compilation of the material used in this text, the author may lay claim to the opinions expressed but not to originality. He is indebted for the knowledge contained herein to experience, to a small degree; to the master craftsmen, now deceased, who started him off—men who considered making a good clinch too important to be adequately learned in a few months; to the researchers and writers from long ago who left such a rich heritage; and to contact with farriers and veterinary practitioners whose rich experience has been drawn upon freely.

R.G.G.

Introduction

Not many years ago the horse seemed to be, as many lamented, "on the way out." His numbers decreased year by year as the internal combustion engine became more numerous and more versatile. The United States Government dropped horses and mules from the census, and Missouri, famous for being the world's foremost source of high-quality mules, terminated the showing of mules at the State Fair.

Car, truck and tractor, as the years went by, nearly displaced the working horse and mule, but recent years have amply demonstrated that the human species is not willing to abandon its equine friend and ally. Horses are increasing in number and popularity each year, besides enjoying an elevation in status. Earlier their value was primarily utilitarian; now they have also become companions of leisure time, and both rider and horse share in the execution of specialized skills.

The horse has a double character. He is an animal admirably adapted to the wild state and equally adapted to the confinement and responsibilities of domestication. The same statement cannot be made for his feet, for they belong to the wild horse in his native prairies and foothills, where they function superbly. When man changed his equine friend's environment, he soon found the feet to be a source of vexation, and the difficulties still continue. The hooves grow too long; on pavement and rocks they wear off faster than they grow; they grow unevenly; the hooves split and crack; the feet are vulnerable to disease. These problems are as modern as they were ancient.

The story of man's attempts through the ages to temper the ills imposed on horses' feet by unnatural living conditions has been assembled piecemeal by historians from works of art, occasional references in literature and the uncovering of artifacts. Leisering and Hartman were among these historians. The following brief outline, extracted from their account as translated by Dollar,* is presented here as a basis for comment.

The ancient Greeks and Romans brilliantly pioneered in many fields of knowledge, but they did not improve the state of the feet of their horses. Alexander the Great accomplished a great deal in a very few years; it does not seem likely that many limits were placed on his activities. Yet his horses' feet apparently hindered him. It is known that he had to abandon great numbers of lame horses in Asia.

The Romans developed the "hipposandal," a metal protective device that was strapped to the limbs of horses. It is thought that the use of hipposandals was reserved for sore-footed animals, although it appears that chafing from the straps created a new problem.

As the Romans overran Europe they encountered many tribes they considered barbaric in spite of substantial development by some in such fields as agriculture, shipbuilding and the arts. A few of the Celtic, Gallic and Germanic tribes conquered by the Romans had been nailing metal shoes on horses since pre-Christian times. But the Romans could not seem to learn, for the

* Dollar, J. A. W., M.R.C.V.S.: A Handbook of Horseshoeing. London, William R. Jenkins, 1898.

only artifacts of hoof-gear found in their European forts have been the hipposandals.

The Mongols claimed that they had been shoeing their tough little horses since very early times. They used a modified type of bar shoe and attached it with three clips. These shoes must have given them some history-making advantage over Alexander, for when they went plundering, they did not stop until they reached Eastern Europe. Alexander did not cross India.

The Arabs, of course, were always noted for the great care they gave to their fine horses. They were using a shoe much like that of the Mongols, attached with nails, before Rome became an empire.

During the Dark and Middle Ages horseshoeing became widespread throughout Continental Europe, Scandinavia and Britain. The shoes were of many types, but crude, and were nailed crudely. They may have prevented wear of the hooves but did little else of benefit. Awkward contraptions used by the Scandinavians were apparently intended to prevent slipping on ice, and probably succeeded—at great expense to the hooves.

The first writing on the subject of horseshoeing was done by several Italians in the 16th century, and so to Italy goes credit for being the founding place of systematic shoeing.

During the 18th century, when the anatomy and physiology of horses' feet were first scrutinized scientifically, the way was paved for the development of scientific shoeing. In the 19th century art and science waxed apace amid the clamor of controversy, trial and error. Several prominent farriers, European and American, were influential in exploiting the new knowledge, but most of the leadership emerged from the veterinary colleges. The French were diverted by unsuccessful experiments; the Germans, British and Americans made the most solid contributions.

Military interests, especially the German, were most vociferous in demanding more effective shoeing. Armies were horse-powered;

the army with the least crippled horses was the more mobile and had a decided advantage over its opponent. In Germany the training of army farriers rested with the veterinary colleges, and in Germany examination and certification of farriers first developed.

By about 1900 horseshoeing reached its status as an art and a science, but the full benefits of the knowledge were slow in filtering through to the many working shops. The shoeing of oxen became an ancillary enterprise, although very few farriers seemed to enjoy this work.

Our older citizens remember when the shoeing shop was necessary to maintenance of mobility and economy. In small town and city the shop was a bustling scene of activity as well as a gathering place for those with time on their hands. With the arrival of the first snow and ice of winter came "sharpening time," when draft animals, and others, were presented in great numbers to be fitted with shoes equipped with sharp calks. This must have been an event welcomed by the proprietors and dreaded by the workers.

Unruly and green horses, which were part of a day's routine, received no great largess of patience. If the discipline demanded by voice and rasp-clout were not forthcoming, ropes were put to use, or a stock. A horse suspended in a stock, feet off the ground, was placed at a great disadvantage in venting his ill temper or displaying his fear. At any rate, an animal was not allowed to use much more than his allotted time on the floor. Too, the farriers worked at a dangerous trade, and no one was likely to assume responsibility for their injuries.

Permanent shoeing shops still exist but are few. The modern farrier has turned to the traveling shop, usually a pickup truck modified in some way to suit the operator's personal preferences, and travels to his clients. It could be said that at this point the gasoline engine, instead of replacing the horse, has in a way become his servant.

Man has come far, quite slowly, in learning to care for his

friend's feet. At some time in the future the attainments we are so proud of today may seem unsophisticated and primitive. If the horse continues to benefit, this is as it should be.

To be well-rounded as a horseman, one must be intimately acquainted with the anatomy, or structure, as well as the needs of a horse's feet. To know less is to be only partly a horseman. To trim, fit shoes and drive nails into the feet, it is absolutely essential to know the anatomy.

Understanding the anatomy of the foot, preventing undue wear of the wall, preventing cracking and splitting of the wall, correcting or improving faults of gait and stride, treating pathological conditions and, when needed, increasing traction — all comprise the objectives of horseshoeing. The same list might well define the science of shoeing, provided that there is the least possible interference with the function of the foot.

The manual and mental skills necessary to choose the most appropriate shoe, prepare the foot correctly for it, and then fit and nail it faultlessly fulfill the requisites of an art.

This know-how and ability have been hard-won by mankind, and are no easy accomplishment for an individual. It is most sincerely hoped that those who wish to enrich their knowledge of horsemanship or to develop a working facility in foot management will find the following pages of value.

Contents

Chapter One

ANATOMY
OF THE
FOOT

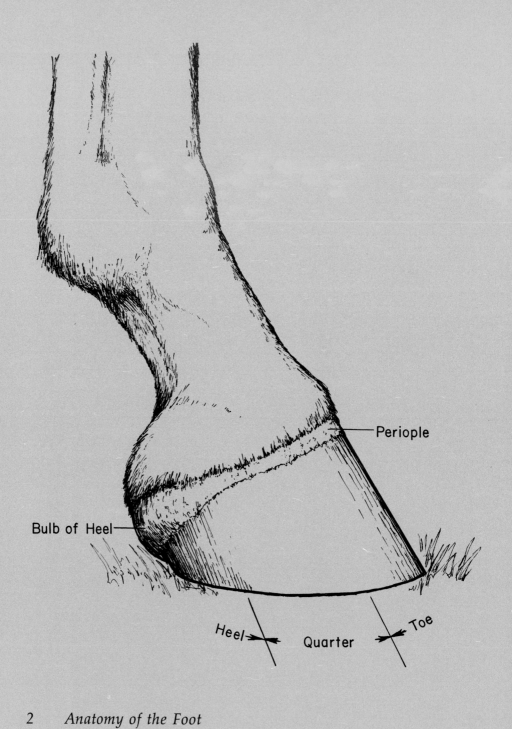

Periople

Bulb of Heel

Heel → ← Quarter → ← Toe

2   *Anatomy of the Foot*

The Hoof

The *hoof* is the horny covering of the foot. The term *foot* includes the hoof and its contents. The parts of the hoof are: wall, bars, bulbs of the heels, sole and frog. The topographic parts of the wall are: toe, quarter and heel. The upper border of the wall at the hairline is called the *coronet*. Just below the coronet is the strip of *periople*, which may correspond to the human cuticle. Toward the heel the periople widens to cover the bulbs of the heels. The function of the periople is to produce the waxy coating on the hoof wall.

Most of the ground surface of the foot is covered by the *sole*. The sole of a well-formed foot is concave. The junction of the sole with the outer wall is the *white line*. The wall has an outer pigmented layer and an inner unpigmented layer; the division into layers may be imperceptible in a "white" hoof. It is erroneous to refer to the inner unpigmented layer as the "white line."

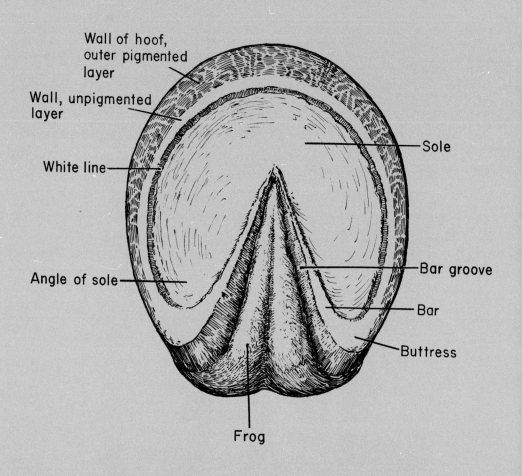

Wall of hoof, outer pigmented layer

Wall, unpigmented layer

White line

Angle of sole

Sole

Bar groove

Bar

Buttress

Frog

The wall is thickest at the toe, becomes thinner at the quarter, and thinner yet at the heel. At the back of the heel the wall turns inward and forward to form the *bar*, which meets the bar of the opposite side at an acute angle. The sharp turn made by the wall is called the *buttress*. The part of the sole between heel and bar is called the *angle* of the sole. The *frog* occupies the triangle formed by the convergence of the bars and is separated from the bars by *grooves*. The frog is continuous behind with the *bulbs* of the *heels*.

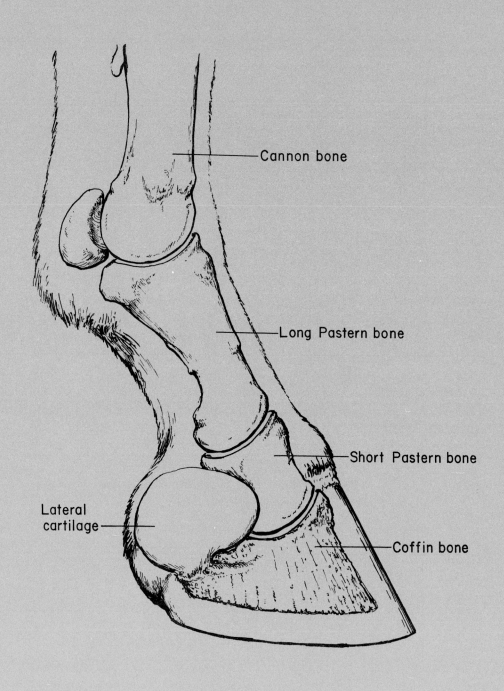

Cannon bone

Long Pastern bone

Short Pastern bone

Lateral cartilage

Coffin bone

6　　*Anatomy of the Foot*

The bones of the foot are presented schematically. The *coffin bone* (third phalanx) is entirely enclosed by the hoof. About one half of the *short pastern bone* (second phalanx) is enclosed by the hoof. The *navicular bone,* not shown, is also within the hoof. Attached to the angle of the coffin bone and directed upward is the *lateral cartilage*. Notice that the lateral cartilage extends well above the coronet, forming the contour of the heel.

The historic term "lateral cartilage" is misleading in that the name does not denote that the structure is paired—there is also a medial lateral cartilage. Substitute names have been proposed, which usually have been too wordy or inaccurate. The author prefers a change to a simple descriptive name such as "heel cartilage" or "expansion cartilage."

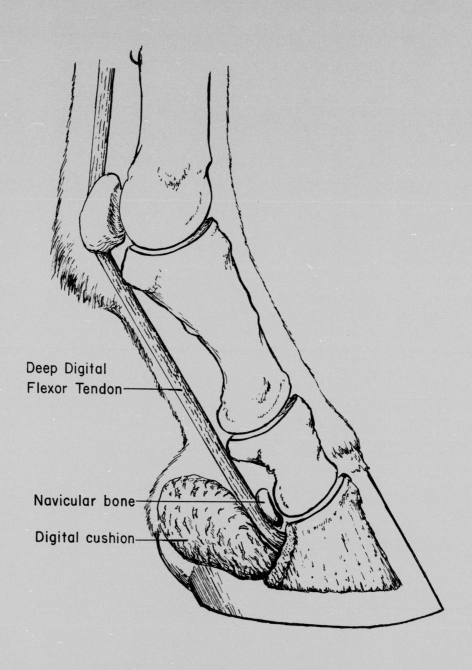

Deep Digital
Flexor Tendon

Navicular bone

Digital cushion

If the angle of the coffin bone and the lateral cartilage were removed, the fibroelastic *digital cushion* would be visible. The digital cushion lies above the frog and part of the sole, between the lateral cartilages and angles of the coffin bone, and below the deep flexor tendon and navicular bone.

Skin is composed of the tough dermis, or *corium*, and a thin cellular covering, the *epidermis*. Below the coronet the epidermis is represented by the horny hoof, while the corium lines the hoof. The corium adheres to the periosteum (outer covering) of the coffin bone; the coffin bone is shaped to fit very snugly within the hoof.

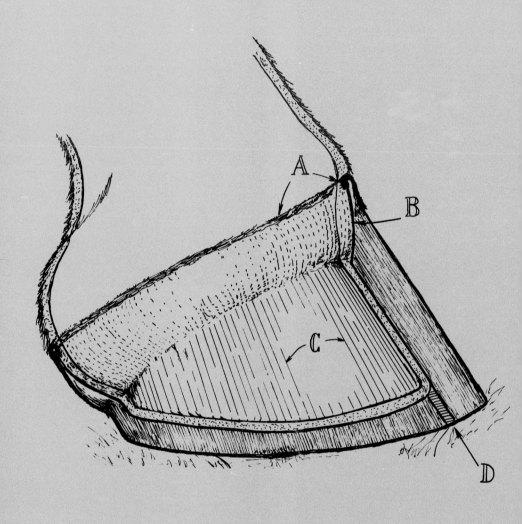

The wall of the hoof just below the coronet is very thin. The inside surface forms a narrow, shallow groove which contains a specialized part of the corium called the *periople* (A). Below the perioplic groove the wall thickens, forming the *coronary groove* (B), which is occupied by a thickening of the corium, the *coronary corium*. The coronary corium produces the wall of the hoof. The wall grows downward from this tissue of its origin in a manner comparable to that of a fingernail. From the bottom of the coronary groove to the ground the wall has a uniform thickness although, as previously stated, the thickness varies with the region of the foot.

The inner surface of the wall is molded into a series of thin ridges which reach from the coronary groove to the ground. These are the rigid *horny lamina* (C). Interlocking with these ridges are corresponding ridges of the corium, the *sensitive lamina*. The sensitive lamina are rich in tiny blood vessels and nerve endings; this is the *quick*. The layer of quick is represented externally by the white line (D).

The corium turns under the coffin bone and becomes responsible for production of the horn of the sole. The sole does not grow from a prescribed region, as does the wall; its growth is uniform in all parts of the sole. The corium and sole do not adhere by lamina, as is the case in the wall; tiny papillae, or projections, from the corium into the sole anchor the horn of the sole in place.

The frog is also lined and produced by corium, and the same can be said of the bulbs of the heels.

Physiology of the Foot

When the foot hits the ground, the burden is transmitted from the frog to the digital cushion and clear up to the withers through an elaborate series of structures designed by nature to absorb concussion. The digital cushion itself, pressing from inside out, forces expansion of the flexible lateral cartilages and the thin walls of the heels.

A great volume of blood circulates through the foot during a given time. The arterial blood, for the most part, enters deeply, whereas the veins, which form an extremely extensive plexus, are more or less superficial. When weight is placed on the digital cushion, it compresses the veins in the vicinity of the heels and lateral cartilages. This forces the contents of the veins up the limb while damming the flow into the compressed region. When weight is removed from the digital cushion, the dammed-up blood rushes into the empty vessels to be forced up the limb at the next step. Since the veins of the lower limbs have no valves to prevent back-flow, flexible heels and exercise are necessary to provide the pumping action so vital to the maintenance of adequate circulation of the feet.

The hoof wall is provided with hollow, vertical cylinders, microscopic in size, for maintenance of moisture in the horn. The waxy coating on the wall secreted by the periople acts to seal the moisture in. If, due to scraping or indiscriminate rasping, the protective coating is lost, the horn tends to dry out and become cracked and brittle. Several commercial products and many home formulations are available for replacing the deficient secretion. Linseed oil works well. Hereafter, these substances will be collectively termed "hoof dressing."

For the health of his feet a horse should be allowed to roam barefoot at pasture, exposed to moisture, for part of each year. If this practice is not feasible, his feet deserve extra attention.

Chapter Two

HANDLING

THE

FEET

To approach, grasp, raise and hold a horse's foot correctly and safely cannot be learned by reading. Competent demonstration plus many awkward, strenuous hours of practice are requisite to mastery of the technique. Nevertheless, the procedures will be briefly outlined in the hope that printed instructions may shorten the learning time.

As with other athletic endeavors, such as bowling and golf, coordination must be trained into the entire body. The objectives are to become able to raise, then hold the foot solidly enough to work on it while feeling relatively comfortable and at ease. Both hands must be free to work. The horse, also, must be comfortable and at ease.

Working with horses' feet always entails some risk of injury, and this includes occasions when one is working with the most gentle of horses. Learning how to protect one's self from injury every second is one of the main objectives of training.

18   Handling the Feet

The Forefoot

To lift the left forefoot, approach from the side. Place the right hand on the horse's shoulder, and the left hand on the front of his fetlock joint or just above. Shift his weight to his right foot; raise the left foot. Turn, facing backward. Straddle the foot; shuffle back and forth till you find the place where you and the horse are comfortable while his foot is held solidly between your knees.

20   *Handling the Feet*

To work on the side of the foot (i.e., clinching nails) carry the foot in front of the horse. Place the frog on your right knee; then move back and forth till you find the place where your knee is comfortable, and you can clamp his toe with your left knee to hold the foot firmly.

To work on the outer side of the foot, face the opposite direction and repeat the procedure. Avoid entanglement with the lead rope.

Raising and holding the right forefoot is, of course, the same operation in reverse.

22   *Handling the Feet*

24   *Handling the Feet*

The Hindfoot

Approach the left hindfoot from the side, and slightly ahead of it. Stand an arm's length away. This will probably keep you out of reach of the foot.

Place the left hand on the point of the hip, keeping the arm stiff. Move the right hand slowly down the limb to, or near, the fetlock.

Shift the horse's weight to his right foot while raising the left foot to your knees. Clamp the toe between your knees. In working with an inexperienced horse, remain in this position a few moments until his confidence in you builds up.

This operation may not have gone as smoothly as the description. Your left elbow is the key to your safety. Keep it firm. Even when you must bend it, keep it firm. If the horse should resist, he will give you advance warning through your left hand. If he decides to kick, the movement of the hip tends to push you aside—if your elbow is firm.

Providing that all went smoothly and his foot is on your right knee, grasp the toe with your right hand and flex the pastern. As long as you maintain flexion, you have control. Turn backward, place his fetlock against your left knee and take short steps backward, keeping the right foot slightly advanced.

Should he fight back vigorously at this point, you have three advantages: the flexed foot and pastern limit his movements, the fetlock against your knee tends to push you aside, and your left hand remains on the point of his hip as long as it can, the elbow still firm.

28   *Handling the Feet*

Move backward until his cannon is about vertical. This will usually place you so that you can hold the front of the foot and fetlock firmly on your knees while freeing both hands. For added solidity, rest your armpit over his hock. Remember, the horse and you must both be comfortable: if you hold his foot too high, he won't cooperate with you very long. You'll probably have to bend your knees.

30   *Handling the Feet*

To clinch nails, move the foot forward much as you did with the front foot. Put his foot on your right knee and clamp his toe with your left knee.

32   *Handling the Feet*

To work on the outside of the foot, either place his foot on your left knee and face more toward his head, or reverse your position and stand between foot and flank, facing outward. If you choose the latter position, be careful not to lean against his flank, or even brush against the flank of mules or flighty horses.

Reverse the procedure for the right foot.

Chapter Three

TRIMMING

THE

HOOF

The object of trimming horses' hooves is to remove excess wall and to balance the foot and stride. Superfluous wall on an unshod foot tends to break off unevenly, a circumstance which could unbalance the stride, cause a chip to break off into the quick, or, because of the uneven breaking, make the wall vulnerable to cracking. Periodic balancing during an animal's growth, starting at a very young age, may help to preserve straightness of limb or help to correct a congenital defect.

Before picking up a foot, observe the feet on the ground and reflect on how they should look after they have been trimmed. The toe of the forefoot should form an angle of 49°, or a trifle less, with the ground; the angle of the hindfoot should be about 54°. A farrier sometimes uses an instrument to measure the angle, but if the angle of the toe is in alignment with the angle of the pastern, it is fairly certain to be right.

The wall of the heel (not the bulbs) parallels the wall of the toe in an ideal foot, although many horses have "cut-under" heels.

The tools required for hoof trimming are a hoof nipper, hoof knife and a rasp. A leather apron is a great comfort to the knees and a protection for the clothing. The apron should be plain. It should be secured by thongs wrapped around the waist and tucked in, never tied. There are occasions when it is vital that the apron be shed in a hurry. An example might be that while a nail is being driven, it emerges from the hoof and penetrates the apron at the same time as a foot gets out of control. Straps, buckles and decorations have no place on a working apron.

Pick up a foot. Clean the sole and grooves with the hoof knife. There will probably be no need to pare the sole of a healthy foot as Nature has a way of shedding the excess horn. Scrape away enough of the loose flakes to determine accurately the amount of excess wall to be removed. If shiny horn begins to appear, live vascular tissue is only a small fraction of an inch away.

The frog seldom needs trimming. It is there for a vital purpose, and again Nature provides for shedding of the excess. One may find it necessary to notch the corners if they interfere with the solid seating of a shoe.

There are instances in abnormal and unhealthy feet in which the sole or frog needs to be pared. Consultation with a veterinarian or farrier should be sought if such a situation is suspected.

Unless the bars are grown out and bent over, do not pare them. To do so weakens the foot.

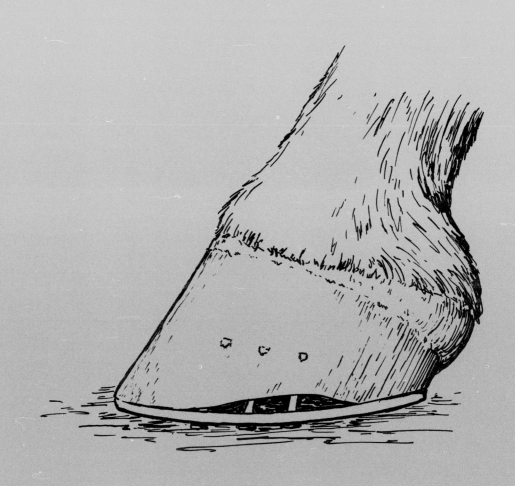

38   *Trimming the Hoof*

Excess wall is removed with the nippers. The cut is made with the jaws parallel with the ground surface, not at right angles to the wall. But first, sight down the foot and determine the course of action. The heels should be equal in height. Be conservative in cutting away the heels; they usually grow slower than the toe. At the toe, the wall is cut level with the sole. Remember that the sole is concave. When the nippers approach the quarters, leave the wall a little longer in order to avoid this finished product:

Smooth and level the wall with a rasp. Frequent sightings are necessary to achieve perfect balance and symmetry. The finished product resembles this:

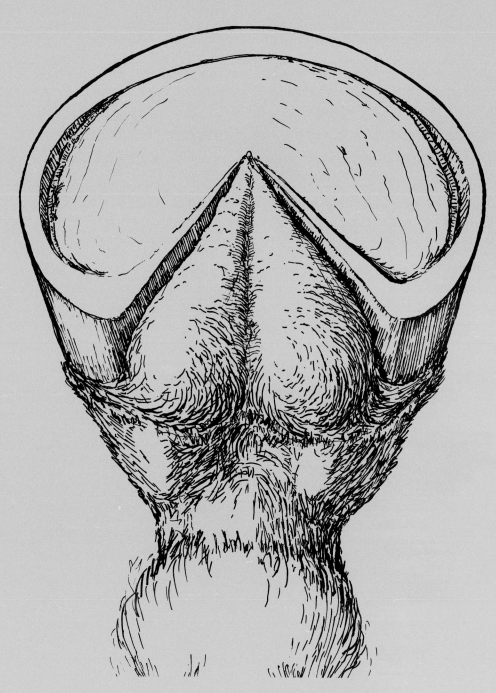

40   *Trimming the Hoof*

The heels are equal in length. The wall is level; it is not cut even with the sole at the quarters. The frog points to the center of the toe—evidence that inside and outside walls are equal in length. Now put the foot on the ground and check the angle. If the toe is not in alignment with the pastern, a little more heel or toe may have to be removed. Make sure both feet of a pair match.

If the foot is not to be shod, leave the wall 1/8 inch longer. Round off the sharp outer edge with the rasp, as this will help to prevent chipping or breaking of the wall. This is an especially good practice if a shoe has just been removed, and the wall is weakened by nail holes.

Often when a horse has been barefooted at pasture, the wall will flare out at the bottom. In this case the flare must be dressed off until the hoof is shaped as it *should* be before a shoe is fitted. This is probably the only situation in which it could be said that the foot is made to fit the shoe, rather than the reverse.

Chapter Four

CORRECTIVE TRIMMING

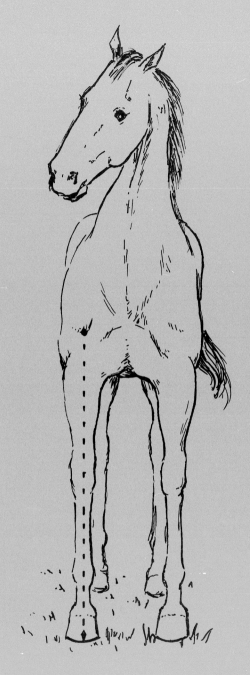

Corrective Trimming

Corrective trimming is performed with the object of improving the stride or gait. Some pathologic conditions are treated by trimming in a special way; this will be discussed in Chapter 8, Therapeutic Shoeing.

A sound horse with good conformation and healthy, well-balanced feet will travel straight and true. Unfortunately, not all horses are sound or well-constructed. This chapter will deal with improvements we can make in a horse's performance by trimming.

There are limitations on trimming in the correction of gait and stride. The position of a horse's foot on the ground may reflect the conformation of the rest of the limb, even the width of the chest. A plumbline dropped from the point of the shoulder of a well-formed horse divides the limb, each joint, and the foot into equal halves. If the foot is not on plumb, look for deviation elsewhere in the limb.

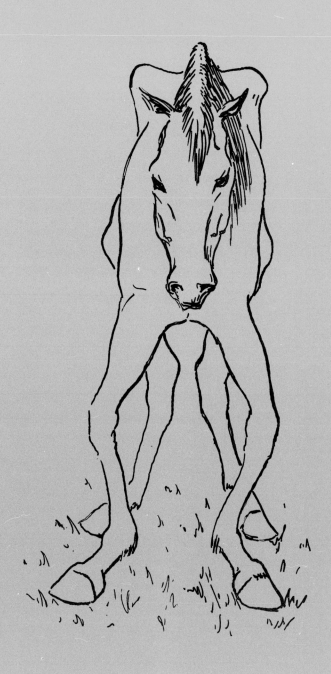

46   *Corrective Trimming*

When a deviation from vertical occurs in a young horse, balancing the foot may help to develop straightness of limb. In a mature horse whose bones and ligaments are fully developed, to balance the foot may throw stress on some of the joints, ligaments and tendons, leading to further woes. Corrective trimming in mature horses should be approached by degrees, or the correction should be accomplished with the use of suitable shoes.

Furthermore, each horse is an individual, and no decision is worthy of acting upon until the horse has been observed in motion. One angular joint may balance another. This horse may travel straight, in which case the wisest decision may be to maintain the unbalanced feet as they are.

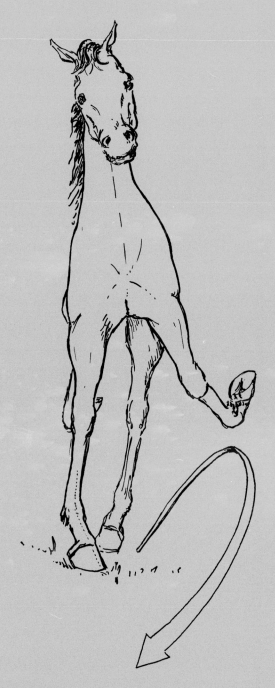

48   Corrective Trimming

Toe-in

One of the faults most commonly encountered is the toe-in position of the feet. Upon examination of the animal we may observe unevenly broken hooves, inferior trimming, a very wide chest or angular joints. Following visual examination the animal is studied in motion. Nearly always we will see a horse that "wings" or "paddles"; that is, his feet travel in an outward arc.

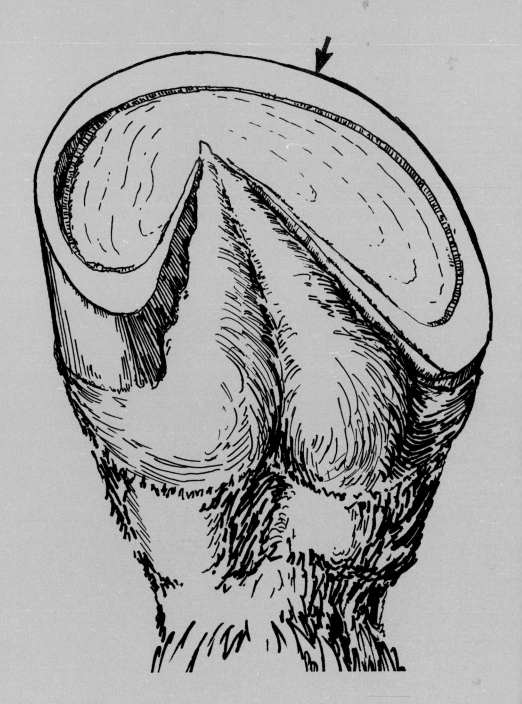

Examination of the bottom of the *left* foot will probably disclose a picture similar to this. The inside wall and heel are longer than the outside. This indicates that he lands on the outside of the foot first, subjecting it to more wear. The frog points to the inside of center, dividing the ground surface of the foot unequally. The foot will break over at the arrow, the lowest point on the toe and therefore the point of least resistance.

In correcting this foot the first consideration is to attempt to establish the correct angle of the foot with the ground. If possible, the heels are made equal in length; then the inside wall and toe are trimmed down. The outside wall is left alone.

Several months of growth and several trimmings may be required to attain a level foot. In the meantime, a light shoe may be necessary to allow growth of the hoof. If desired, some form of corrective shoe could be used.

Corrective Trimming

Toe-out

The toe-out position is the opposite of the condition just described. The horse's feet will most likely travel with an inward arc, or "wing in." When the foot in motion strikes the supporting limb, the act is called "interfering."

Examination may disclose a narrow chest or, again, angular joints, faulty trimming or broken hooves. The bottom of the left foot will probably exhibit a short inside wall and heel. The frog points to the outside of center of the toe.

Again, the desired angle of the foot is determined, and the heels are made as near the same length as the shape of the foot permits. The outside wall and toe are cut down; the inside wall is not disturbed. The precautions and limitations are similar to those that apply to the toe-in position.

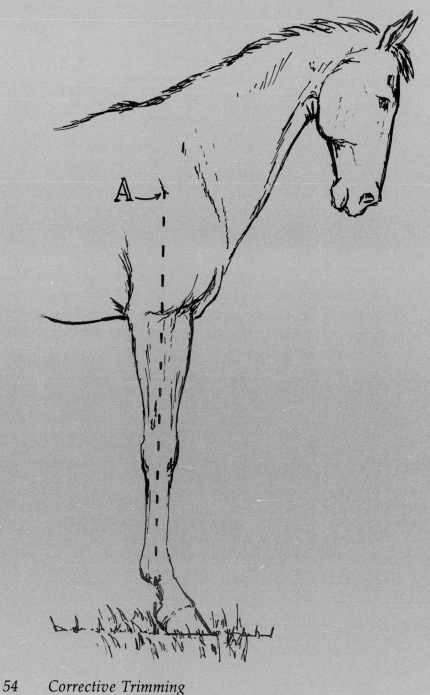

When a plumbline is dropped from the tuber spinae (A) of a horse of good conformation, the line passes through the center of elbow, carpal (knee) and fetlock joints, dividing them equally. Below the fetlock the line passes just behind the bulbs of the heels.

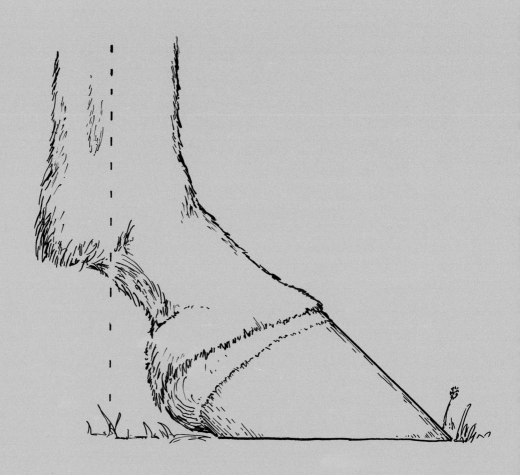

Low Angle

This foot has too long a toe. The condition may have resulted from breaking off of the heels, trimming or inferior conformation. In landing and standing the body weight is centered too far back in the foot, placing inordinate strain on the deep flexor tendon and the suspensory ligament. In action the foot is slow to break over, necessitating a lengthening of stride. The foot travels lower, making the animal subject to stumbling. The foot may pause momentarily at the forward extremity of the stride; this is called "pointing." Loss of synchronization may cause the forefoot to be struck by the hindfoot; this is called "forging."

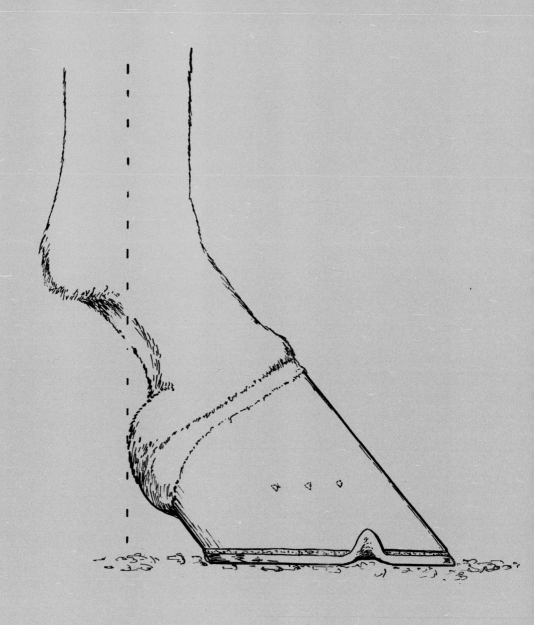

Corrective Trimming

The long-toed foot should not be confused with the long foot, often considered desirable in gaited horses, parade horses and others. The long foot tends to exaggerate action; proper angle and balance are maintained.

The feet of this horse are placed too far forward. The flexor tendons and suspensory ligament are overburdened. The center of gravity of the entire animal moves back; he tries to compensate by advancing the hind feet, but now there is strain on the loin and hocks. The stride is apt to be shortened. When this posture has a sudden onset and cannot be explained by recent faulty foot care, it is well to consult a veterinarian.

Corrective Trimming

The weight in *knee-spring* is definitely on tendons and ligaments. Flexion of knee and foot are not well synchronized. Leave
this horse in the barn when surefootedness is required.

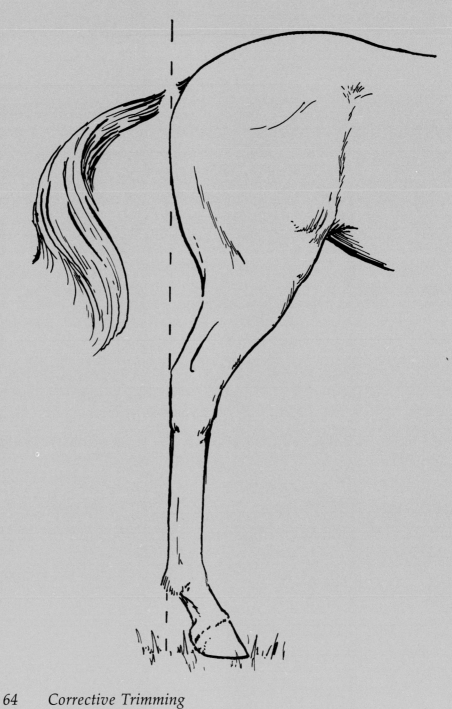

When a plumbline is dropped from the point of the buttock of a well-formed horse, the line touches the back of the hock, parallels the cannon and touches the back of the fetlock. The effects of the overly long toe apply to the hindlimb the same as to the forelimb.

Tennessee Walking Horses are commonly shod with a very low angle in order to slow the breakover and increase the length of stride. The angle of the forefeet is meticulously matched with a suitable angle in the hindfeet to prevent forging.

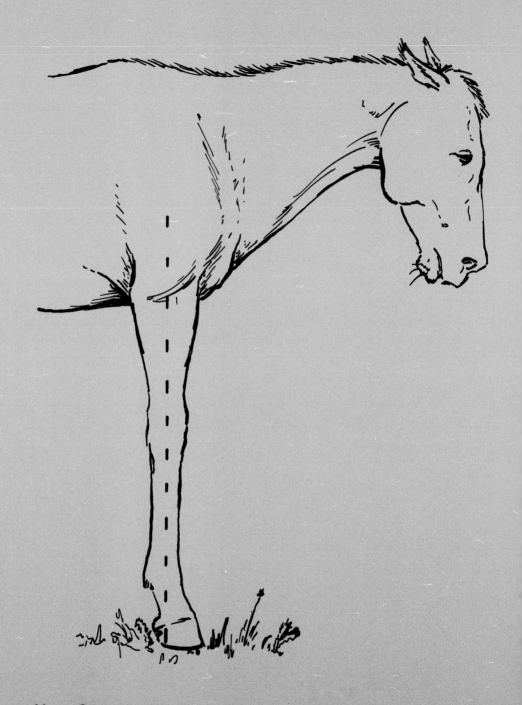

Short Toe

The short toe is usually found on a stubby, upright foot and pastern, and is typically accompanied by a relatively vertical shoulder. The stride is short and choppy, uncomfortable to a rider. If the fault can be attributed to trimming or breaking of the foot, by all means correct it. If the fault is of conformation in a mature horse, proceed very cautiously in changing the angle of the foot by lengthening the toe.

The Shod Horse

For the most part, the preceding conditions have been described as they apply to wear on the bare feet. When a shod horse is being studied, the wear on the shoes will approximate the wear as described for the bare feet in the corresponding conditions.

For instance, the horse that paddles usually lands first on the outside of the foot, wearing it off faster. Accordingly, we may expect to find the outside branch of the shoe he wears more heavily worn off. He probably breaks over on the outside of the toe, again showing more wear on the toe of the shoe at that point.

Judicious trimming within the limits previously described may help. Even the heels, cut down the inside wall and toe, but leave the outside wall and toe longer.

The horse may be further benefited by the application of a corrective shoe, a subject we will soon explore.

Chapter Five

THE SHOE

Horses are shod primarily to prevent inordinate wear of the hoof walls. Shoeing may also be utilized for other purposes, such as improving stride and gait or improving the well-being of an animal.

Shoes do have an effect on the horse. They decrease his speed, agility and endurance. They exaggerate action; in flight the shod foot travels a little higher and a little farther than the same foot unshod. Shoes are capable of seriously interfering with the normal physiologic activities of the feet. Indeed, one of the driving forces in the development of scientific shoeing was the need to protect the wall of the feet without destroying Nature's mechanisms for preservation of the health of the feet. The most scientific and artistic shoeing is only partially successful in realizing this goal.

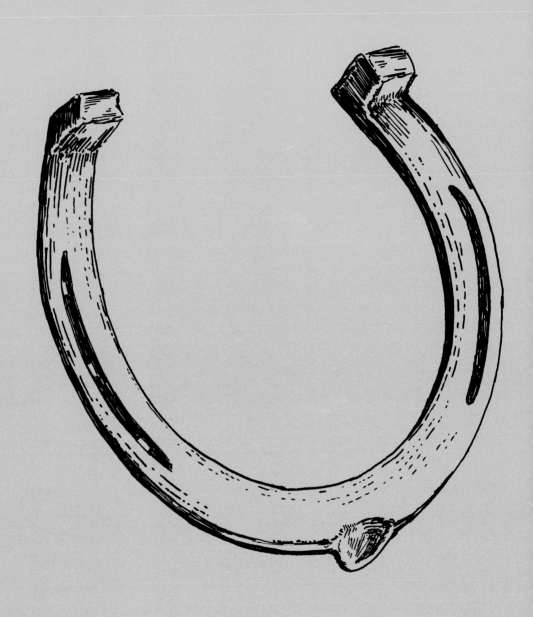

72   *The Shoe*

The shoe itself consists of a toe and two branches, or the parts may be called toe, quarter and heel to correspond with their relation to the hoof. A projection on the ground surface is a "calk." A "clip" is a thin projection, drawn with the hammer from the outside edge of the shoe, that lies against the hoof to give support to the seating of the shoe. The shoe is perforated by nail holes. The nail holes on the ground surface of a machine-made shoe are joined by a groove called a "nail crease"; if the groove is incorporated into a handmade shoe, it is often called "fullering."

The width of the shoe is called the "web." The web should cover the wall, the white line and a narrow strip of sole. The web should be thick enough to support the width and accommodate the head of appropriately sized nails.

Six nails are usually the ideal number for one foot. The nail holes should be so punched that the shanks of the nails fit snugly. The nail crease is punched to afford a firm fit for the nailheads of the size to be used. The nail holes in a handmade shoe may be punched to conform with the varying thickness and slope of the wall; machine-made shoes are more limited in this respect. No nails are driven behind the quarter — nails would weaken the thin wall and inhibit normal flexibility of the heel.

The toe and quarter should fit the foot precisely. A narrow strip of steel should show behind the quarter; this allows for growth of the wall and encourages expansion of the heel. The shoe should project perhaps 1/8 inch behind the heel to allow for growth.

Although heel calks are commonly used, they should probably be reserved for a specific need. They change the angle of the foot, except in the softest ground, and do not appear to be effective in the prevention of slipping.

Chapter Six

NAILING

A

SHOE

This critical part of horseshoeing cannot, certainly, be mastered without firsthand instruction and much practice, but the principles of the art of nailing a shoe may be described. It is unwise to attempt driving nails into a foot until one is thoroughly "at home" holding and handling the foot.

If old shoes are to be removed, one immediately has the opportunity to test his skill at foot-holding. Remove the clinches with a rasp, clinch cutter or nail cutter. The shoe is loosened with pull-off pincers. Tighten the jaws under one branch, then the other. If the nails come loose, it is best for the hoof if they are pulled one at a time. If the heads remain wedged in the nail crease, remove them with the shoe. Using short strong strokes with the pincers, progressing equally on both branches, pry the shoe off.

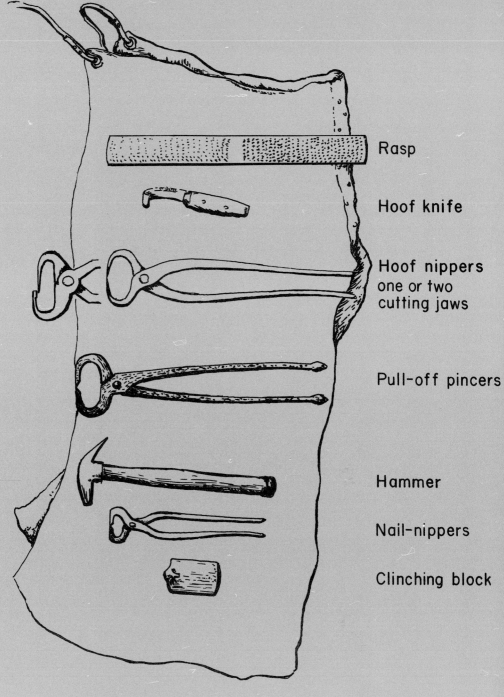

Rasp

Hoof knife

Hoof nippers
one or two
cutting jaws

Pull-off pincers

Hammer

Nail-nippers

Clinching block

78   *Nailing a Shoe*

For applying the shoe, a small hammer made specifically for this purpose should be used. The face may be round or square, depending on preference. A nipper for withdrawing and cutting nails is needed. Some farriers use a clinching block, but nail nippers can be substituted quite adequately. A leather apron is vital to one's safety.

Assuming that the foot is prepared for the shoe and the shoe accurately fitted to the foot, it is now time to drive the first nail. The nail hole to be occupied first is a matter of choice, but the first or second hole nearest the hammer hand is probably best. The *flat* side of the nail goes to the *outside*! The point of the nail is beveled in such a way that the point turns outward when the nail is being driven.

In a well-made hand-punched shoe the nail is started deep in the wall near the white line. In a machine-made shoe the placing cannot be so well determined.

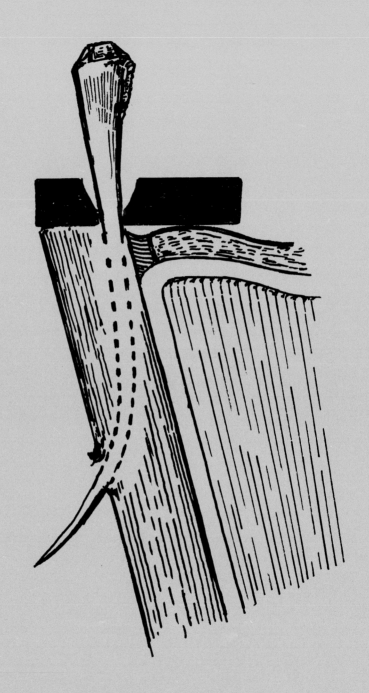

80   *Nailing a Shoe*

Intentions are for the nails to emerge about 3/4 inch from the shoe in a neat row. Several factors influence the success of this venture. One is the proper aiming of the nail in accordance with the slope of the wall. Another is control of the bevel on the nail point; the more firmly the nail is struck, the more the bevel turns the point outward. A solid, dense hoof gives the bevel a chance to work; in a shelly, cracked hoof the course of the nail is less predictable.

A rule of thumb, especially with shallow-punched machine shoes, is to start the nail parallel with the slope of the hoof, but do not hesitate to temper the rule with judgment. Aim the nail with the grain of the hoof. Start with light taps of the hammer — the deeper the nail penetrates, the firmer the blows become.

Don't set the nail head snugly until the second nail has been driven, and you are assured the shoe is satisfactorily in place. However, the point of the nail constitutes a real hazard and must be disposed of promptly. In a shop the points are twisted off with the claw of the hammer. In a barn, or wherever the points may be dangerous to stock or tires, it is best to turn the points down and flatten them against the hoof; then dispose of them while the clinches are being prepared.

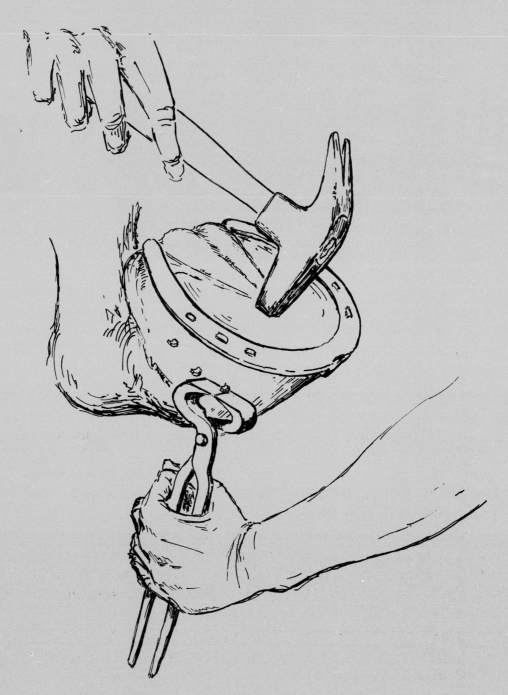

82   *Nailing a Shoe*

When all the nails are driven, "set" them with sharp blows with the hammer. Then place the clinching block (or nail-nippers) under each protruding nail and draw it tight.

To clinch the nails the foot is brought forward and held. The protruding nails are cut to length and rasped square. The clinches should be left long enough for strength but short enough for neatness. When the nail emerges, it displaces a chip of horn. With a light rasp stroke remove the chip from under the nail in order to make as strong a clinch as possible.

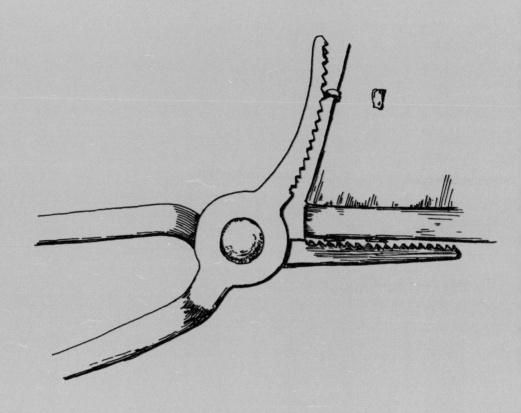

84   *Nailing a Shoe*

To make the clinch a special tool, the "alligator pincer," may be used.

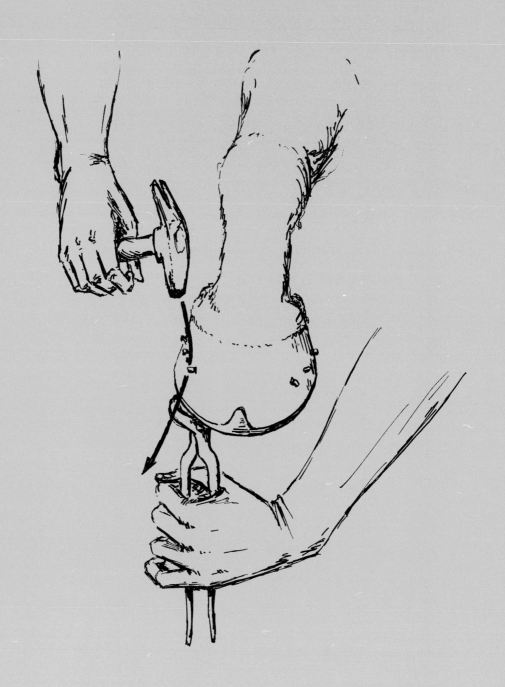

86   Nailing a Shoe

Most farriers prefer the neater clinches they can make with a hammer. Place the clinching block (or nail-nipper) firmly under the nail head. The clinch is hammered down. Direct the hammer in an arc roughly parallel to the hoof wall—direct blows may injure the deep sensitive tissue.

The clinches need to be smoothed with the rasp, but avoid rasping the surface of the hoof and removing the waxy coating.

Use only clean, straight nails. If a nail is rusty, or is extracted after one or two blows, it is false economy to consider it usable.

Occasionally a misdirected nail will "quick" a horse; that is, enter the sensitive tissue. This is painful to the horse, and his response is usually positive. If such an accident is even suspected, leave that nail hole unoccupied. Local treatment and tetanus antitoxin are indicated; it is often best to remove the shoe.

Should a horse go lame shortly after shoeing, it may be that the curvature of a nail crowds the sensitive tissue without actual penetration. Light hammer taps or pressure with nippers usually identifies the offending nail. Remove the nail and examine it for moisture, rust and odor. Whether or not you find them, it is best to treat the nail hole as you would a frank penetration. Unless immediate improvement is obvious, the other nails in the shoe are suspect. Remove the shoe.

Chapter Seven

CORRECTIVE SHOEING

Corrective Shoeing

Effect of Weights

It has been agreed previously that weight attached to a foot affects the movement of that foot. It follows then that it is possible to change the stride by manipulation of the distribution of weight on the foot.

Toe Weight

An unbalanced shoe with the preponderance of weight at the toe tends to increase the length of stride. Toe-weighted shoes are popular for use with gaited horses, fine harness horses, walking horses and others.

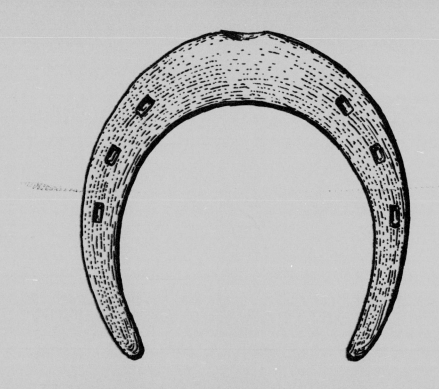

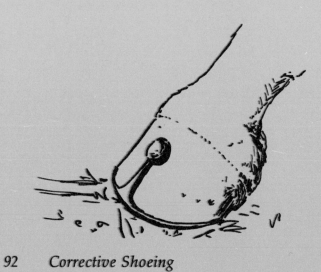

92   *Corrective Shoeing*

Most toe-weighted shoes are handmade, but they can be improvised from a factory shoe.

Very light shoes are desirable on trotters and pacers; and so when a trainer wishes to lengthen an animal's reach, he employs a removable weight attached to a long toe clip.

Use of a toe-weighted shoe is one way to lengthen the choppy stride of the horse with short toe and stubby, upright pastern.

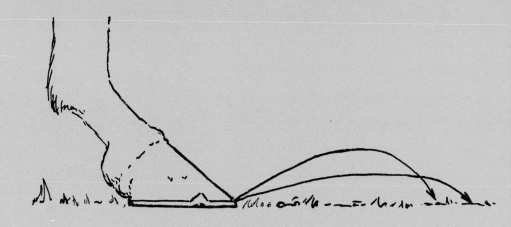

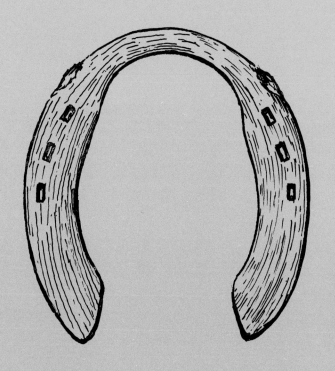

Heel Weight

An unbalanced shoe with a heavy heel tends to increase flexion, or height of action of the limb. Most heel-weighted shoes are handmade, but they can be improvised from factory shoes. The bar shoe is in effect a modified heel-weighted shoe.

Heel weights may be used for correction of stumbling or pointing. The long-toed foot accompanied by an overly sloping pastern is likely to benefit from heel weights.

Side Weights

The mechanical principle behind the use of side weights for straightening the stride can be illustrated with buckets.

Two empty buckets being carried tend to hang vertically.

If a brick were placed on the inside of each bucket, the ground surface would turn outward.

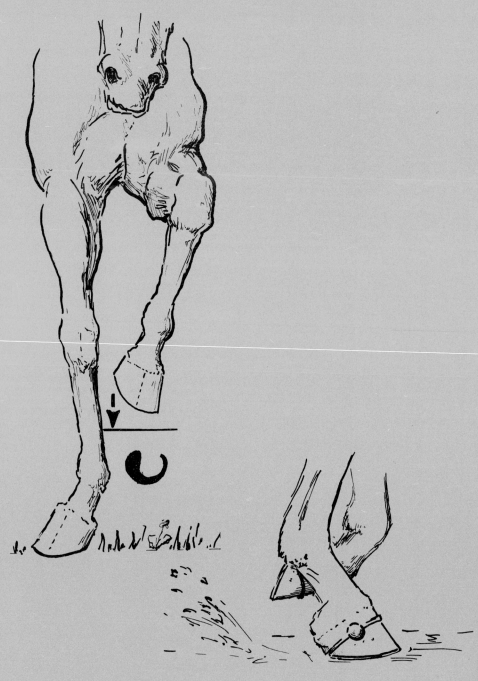

98   *Corrective Shoeing*

To apply this principle to the feet of a horse, use a toe-out horse for an example. If heavy weights were applied to the inside of the foot, the foot would be expected to travel more nearly level in flight.

With some animals the use of side weights is quite successful. However, mechanical principles notwithstanding, the effect of side weights is not too predictable. They often seem to work in reverse. When they are being tried, secure them with two or three nails and observe the action of the animal. If the effect is wrong, reverse the shoes.

The principle of side weights commonly works in reverse on the hindlimbs. Trotters and pacers that "travel narrow" behind are often equipped with removable weights strapped to the outside of the feet.

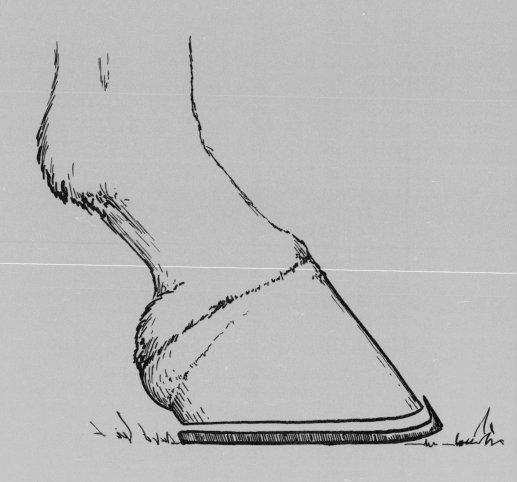

Shoes Used to Straighten the Stride

Innumerable shoes have been developed whose purpose is to straighten the stride. Most of them are variations of a few standard types that have proven popular and effective.

Roller-motion Shoe

Rasp a curvature on the toe of the foot, and then curve the shoe to fit the foot.

The roller-motion shoe is quite effective in forcing the foot to break over at the center of the toe — or at another point, if desired.

The toe of the shoe only can be rounded with grindwheel or on the anvil to supply limited roller motion.

A side effect of the shoe is that it eases and speeds the break-over, thus shortening the stride.

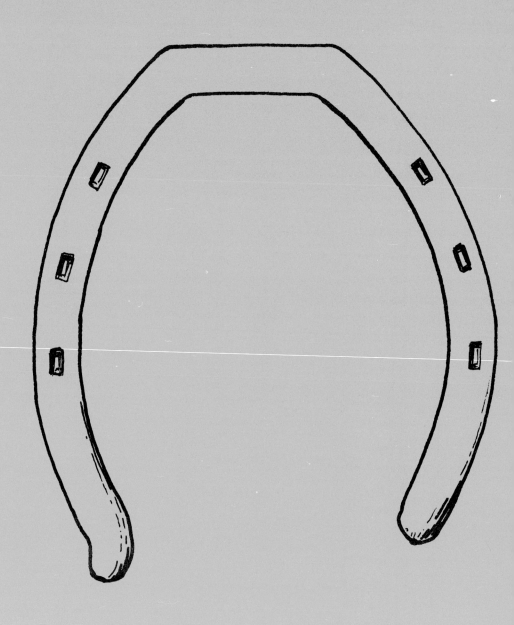

Square Toe

A square toe can enforce a straight breakover. This type of shoe is more suited to the hind feet. It could be criticized for removing some of the bearing from the wall. Again, the breakover is speeded and the stride shortened.

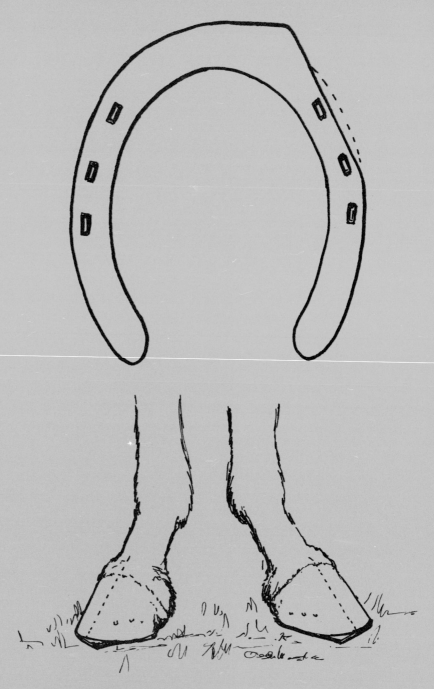

Corrective Shoeing

The Lateral Extension Shoe

The word "lateral" in the name of this shoe is a misnomer, as the extension can be either lateral or medial.

The extension is applied at the point the foot breaks over, forcing the breakover point to the center of the toe.

An added feature in the single shoe illustrated is the receded outline behind the extension. If the horse should continue to interfere in spite of the shoe, he will hit the other limb with his hoof rather than with steel.

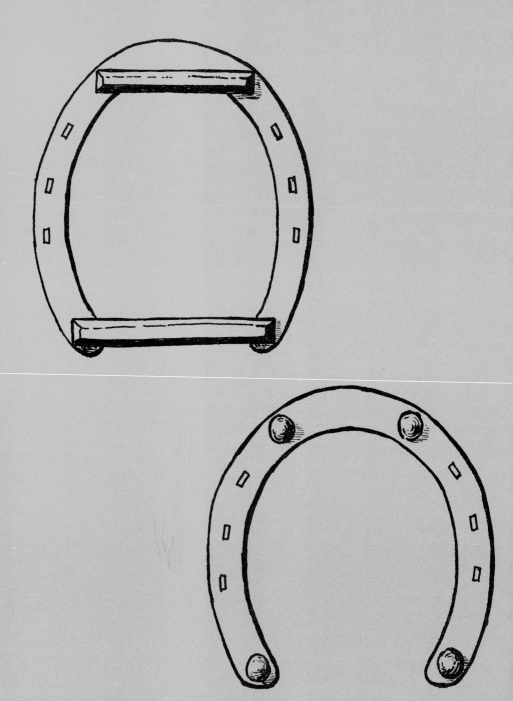

The Memphis Bar or Memphis Calk

This shoe works better on hard surfaces. It was developed for draft horses working on pavement, but it can be useful in some situations for light horses. The bar, or calks, at the toe can be moved forward or back to change the length of stride and ease of breakover. If need be, the bar, or calks, at the toe can be set at an angle to control further the point of breakover.

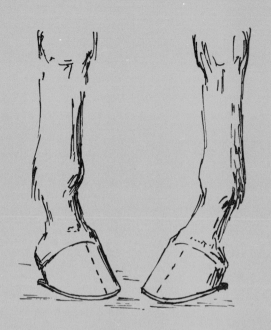

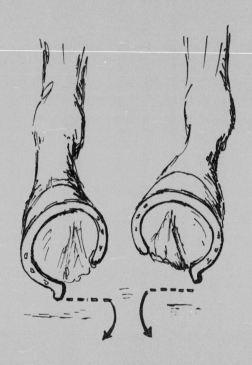

Trailers

A trailer, or elongated branch, is put on the heel that hits the ground first. This gives the other heel a chance to catch up. To increase the effectiveness of a trailer, a short calk may be added.

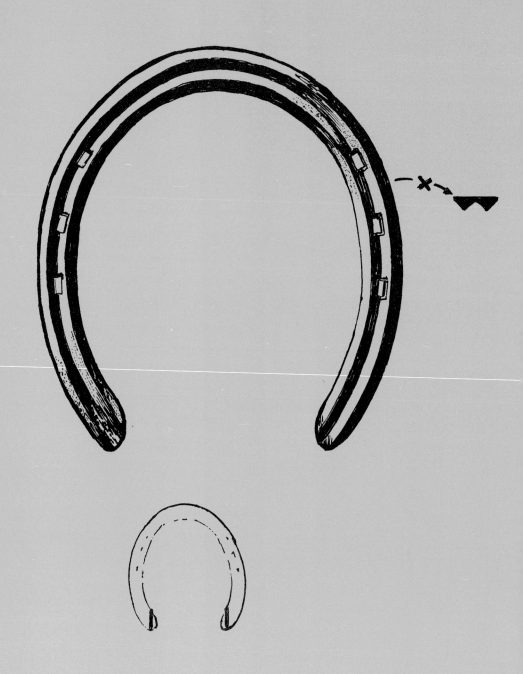

The Racing Shoe

The double rimmed racing shoe was designed for reduction of weight without much loss of strength. It supplies a good grip on the ground. It is attached to the hoof with very small nails.

Sometimes narrow heel calks are used with racing "plates" to prevent sideslipping on turns. The thin calks do not interfere with the slide.

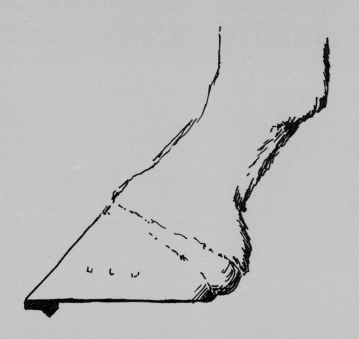

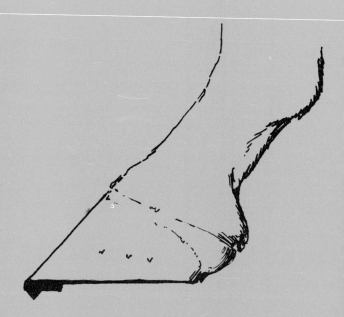

112   *Corrective Shoeing*

The racing plate is a versatile corrective shoe. For instance, if the outer rim is removed at the toe, the shoe can be substituted for a roller-motion shoe, in which capacity it shortens the stride.

If the inner rim is removed, the tendency is toward a lengthened stride.

The precision required in the gait of racing horses may require subtle alterations in the shoes. Racing plates, as well as other shoes, can be equipped with rims, partial rims, calks and grabs varyingly placed to effect specific objectives. Such refinements are prescription treatments for well-studied individual cases. When simpler shoes do not perform satisfactorily, experimentation with these accessories may follow; their effect on the stride is determined by the basic principles already described.

Faults of Gait

Thus far our major attention has been given to the *stride*, the movement of a limb from the time the foot leaves the ground until it lands. The combined movement of all limbs is the *gait*. Needless to say, the quality of the gait is dependent on the satisfactory performance of each limb.

Generally speaking, the faster a horse moves, the more pronounced defects in his gait become. When his movements are being analyzed, he should be observed first traveling at a walk, then at a brisk trot. He should be observed approaching, leaving

and from the side. The movements should be crisp and well coor-
dinated; the flight of the limbs should be straight.

Paddling

Paddling, or "winging out," may be a fault of either fore or hind
feet. It is usually, but not necessarily, observed in a horse whose
toes turn in. When such is the case, corrective measures have been
discussed. If, as sometimes happens, the foot appears level—or
even toes out—corrective trimming may be attempted, but better
results can be expected from corrective shoes. The best shoe may
have to be selected through trial and error; the simpler it is, the
better. First try a trailer on the outside branch, then perhaps an
outside side weight.

Interfering

When a horse is said to interfere, its supporting limb is being
struck by the foot in flight. This is, as we have seen, most likely to
occur among animals with a toe-out stance. If so, corrective trimming and shoes are indicated. If the foot appears level or toes in,
try limited corrective trimming, but depend more on corrective
shoes. Observe the animal carefully at the trot; you will probably
try a short trailer, and perhaps a short calk, on the inside branch.

Forging

When an animal forges, his forefoot is struck by the hindfoot of the same side. Extremely astute observation is required to detect the fault in coordination. The forefeet may break slowly or reach too far. The hindfeet may break too soon or overreach. After meticulous study of fore and hind feet, standing and in motion, try to base corrective measures on adjustment of the angle of the hooves. Judiciously selected shoes may be required.

Forging is often brought on by exhaustion, especially in young horses, and is not to be confused with a true fault of gait. Occasionally a young horse seems to adopt forging as a vice.

Cross-firing

Cross-firing, the striking of a forefoot by the hindfoot of the opposite side, is predominantly a fault of horses that race in harness. Occasionally it is observed in other horses. Correction involves both straightening the stride and changing the coordination between fore and hind limbs.

Others

There are other faults of gait, but most of them can be attributed to the presence of some pathologic condition. When the performance of a horse is less than satisfactory and no obvious explanation is discernible, the wisest course is often to utilize the services of a veterinarian.

Variations and Exceptions

Many general rules have been outlined, but less has been said about the many variations and exceptions. Each horse is an individual and should be so considered; to study him superficially and prescribe by formula may be doing him an injustice.

To this end the ingenuity of many master farriers has been employed. An infinite variety of shoes have been fashioned for all conceivable imperfections of foot, stride and gait. Examination of a collection of corrective shoes can be quite perplexing, but an attempt to analyze the purpose of each shoe is a fascinating adventure.

Chapter Eight

THERAPEUTIC
SHOEING

Corrective shoeing deals with alleviation of congenital or acquired variations from the ideal. *Therapeutic shoeing* is concerned with the treatment of pathologic conditions. The feet of a horse may be ravaged by inexpert care, excessive concussion, poor conformation, unfavorable terrain, trauma, puncture, metabolic disorders or a combination of these. A pathologic condition is usually accompanied by pain, disfigurement or both. It is important to know exactly what is wrong; this may require professional diagnosis by a veterinarian.

The complex structure of the foot and limb of the horse affords many opportunities for disruption of health. A myriad of shoes have been developed to deal with such misfortunes. Some of the more common ailments, those most amenable to treatment by preparation of the foot and shoeing, have been selected for consideration.

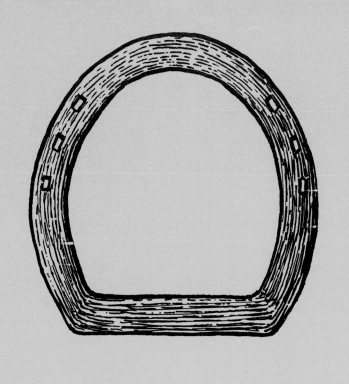

First, a word about the *bar shoe*, probably the most common therapeutic shoe. The heels are joined by a bar. The bar is there to help restore what shoeing often reduces—frog pressure. In terms of weight distribution, the bar shoe is a modified heel weight. There are many variations of the bar shoe; some are designed to afford full frog pressure.

The bar can be curved downward, if desired, to eliminate frog pressure.

Therapeutic Shoeing

Corns

Corns are the result of bruising at the angle of the sole. They most frequently result from leaving shoes on the feet too long. As the hoof grows longer, it becomes larger; the shoe does not. The shoe is drawn forward, leaving the heel to bear on the angle of the sole.

The corns themselves need treatment and must be relieved of weight. For a bare foot, trim the heels short, or notch the wall.

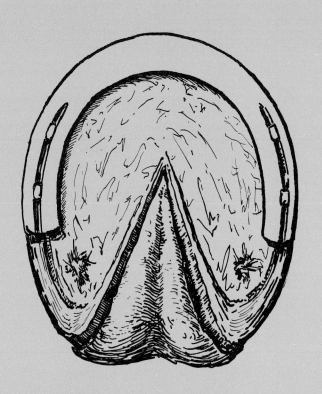

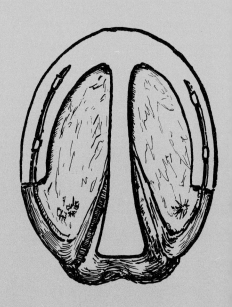

If a shoe is required, use a 3/4 shoe.

In order to maintain frog pressure while using a 3/4 shoe, this type of accessory has been used.

Wall Cracks

Vertical cracks in the wall are unsightly and can lead to serious lameness. Severe cracks may involve the sensitive tissue beneath the wall or extend upward until they involve the germinal tissue of the horn at the coronary band. Cracks in a bare foot may result from excessive growth and uneven breaking off of the wall. In a shod foot, the shoe may have been left in place till the hoof grossly outgrew the shoe. Usually the hoof is in a dried out, unhealthy state; this may have resulted from use of the rasp on the outside of the wall.

The progress of a crack can often be halted with a countergroove. With the rasp, cut a shallow groove at the top of the crack, perpendicular to it. With the nippers, cut a notch in the wall at the ground surface in order to remove bearing from the afflicted part of the wall. This is done whether or not a shoe is to be worn. Apply a hoof dressing to maintain moisture in the hoof and stimulate growth of the horn.

More serious cracks, especially those that cause lameness, may require the expert services of a farrier or veterinarian.

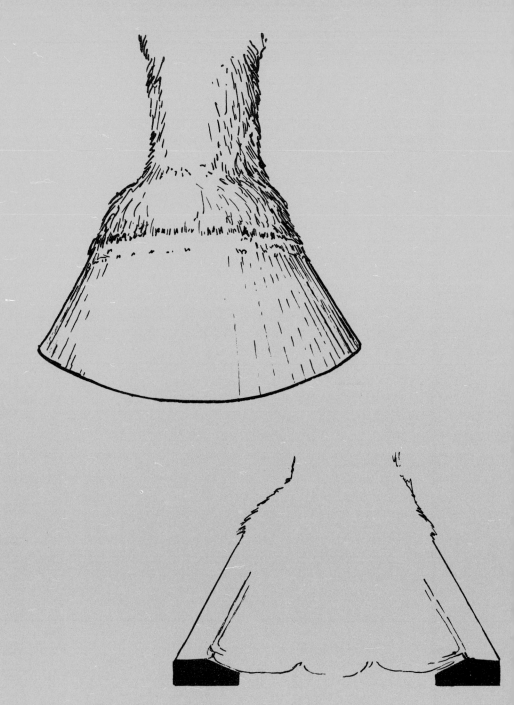

Flat Feet

The term "flat feet" describes a type of poor conformation in which the slope of the hoof is too shallow, especially at the quarters. Concavity of the sole is very shallow or nonexistent.

If an attempt is made to manufacture a sightly foot, the wall is cut too short, leaving the weight of the animal on the sole. When the foot is shod, the shoe presses on the sole. One tends to pare the sole dangerously thin in trying to reduce the size of the foot.

A better alternative is to bevel the inside of the web on the foot surface to accommodate the sole. The bevel may be made on the anvil or with a grindwheel.

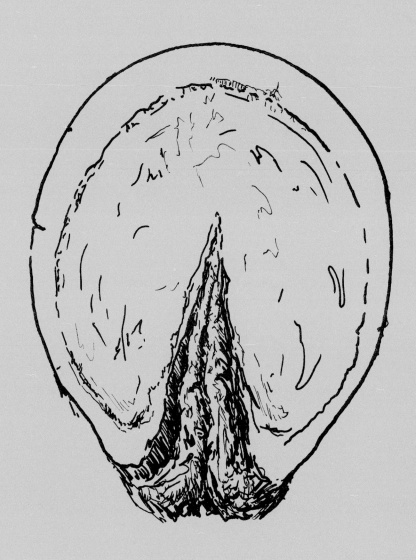

Contracted Heels

Contracted heels are a disfigurement of the foot brought about by dryness of hoof, excess trimming of the frog, ill-advised shoeing, neglect or as a sequel of some other condition. When the physiologic flexibility of the heels is reduced, the concomitant loss of circulation is destructive to the health of the foot. The normal course of a case of contracted heels is to worsen progressively.

If caught early, the feet may respond well to rest at pasture. More advanced cases need help. The use of a bar shoe may be indicated to help restore frog pressure with the attendant benefit of more adequate circulation. Before applying the bar shoe, be very certain that contracted heels are the primary condition; if the heels are contracted as a result of sidebones or navicular disease, the bar is definitely not indicated.

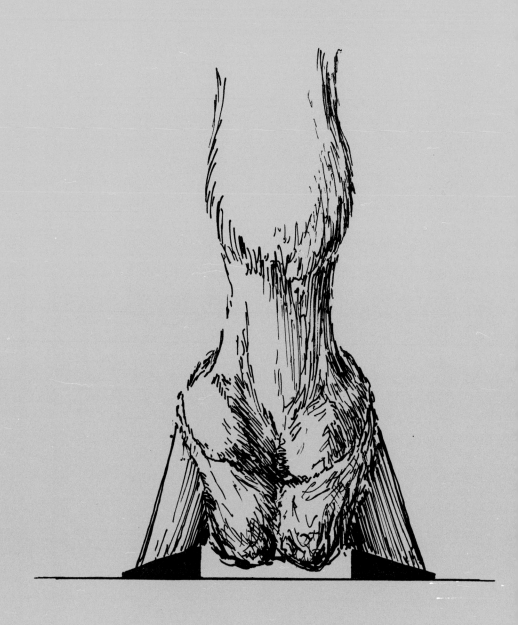

134   *Therapeutic Shoeing*

An effective treatment is to fashion shoes with the web beveled behind the quarter. The bevel is best forged on the anvil, but it may be ground off. The very weight of the horse will force the heels to expand.

Sidebones

Sidebones are ossification (turning to bone) of the lateral cartilages. When the heels above the hairline of a normal foot are pressed between thumb and fingers, they are resilient. If no resilience is detectable in one or both cartilages, ossification can well be diagnosed. Unfortunately, the progress of sidebone is irreversible and usually undetectable until the condition is well advanced.

Sidebones usually result from concussion, as from steady use on pavement or from conditions which interfere with the normal expansion of the heel: dry, unhealthy horn, lack of frog pressure.

Should a case be discovered in its early stages, a bar shoe may be of some benefit. After the cartilages are ossified, a bar shoe is out of order: application of internal pressure through the frog to a foot whose heels are unyielding performs no service to a horse.

The usefulness of a horse with sidebones is more or less limited. Rest at pasture, exposure to moisture and the use of hoof dressing may improve the overall health of the feet. Sidebones often accompany, encourage or result from contracted heels; shoes with the heels beveled may be helpful.

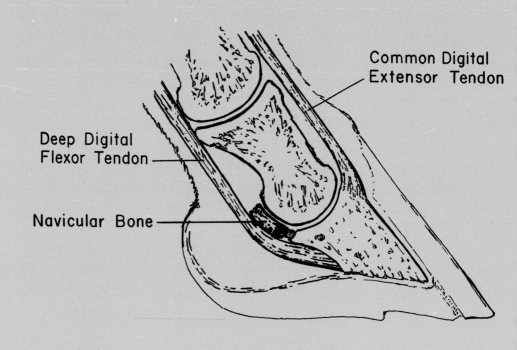

Common Digital
Extensor Tendon

Deep Digital
Flexor Tendon

Navicular Bone

Navicular Disease

Navicular disease is a painful, debilitating condition involving pathology, possibly fracture, of the navicular bone. Its primary cause is probably impairment of circulation in the foot, aggravated by concussion or trauma. Its conclusive diagnosis rests with a veterinarian.

When the foot lands, pain is produced in the posterior part of the foot. Therefore the center of gravity, as the foot lands and stands, should be moved forward nearer the toe. Cut the toe short, leave the heels long. Use a roller-motion or other easy breakover shoe.

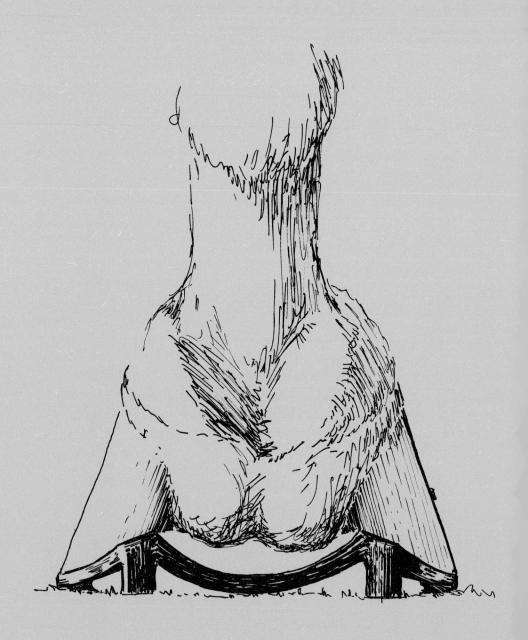

Frog pressure should be reduced to a minimum, a goal which eliminates any consideration for the use of the ordinary bar shoe. However, the bar could be curved downward and balanced with calks, which would be beneficial.

Contracted heels consistently accompany navicular disease; shoes with beveled heels have been given credit for hastening recovery.

Tendinitis

To the horseman tendinitis (inflamed tendons) of the digital flexor muscles are of the most significance. The tendons of these muscles lie behind the cannon, fetlock and pastern. A fluid swelling of the region often accompanies tendinitis, in which case the medical term is "tenosynovitis"; the horseman simply calls it "stocking up." Tendinitis may be severe enough to cause frank lameness. It may be acute or chronic.

Tendinitis often results from wrenching or similar trauma. Overexertion is many times to blame: the horse that stands in a stall all week is not always in adequate physical condition for a rigorous workout on Saturday afternoon. Among gaited horses the application of very heavy shoes sometimes places excessive demands on the tendons. A sudden change in the angle of the feet, such as a drastic lowering of the heel, may overstretch the tendons.

If the inflammation is obviously transient, it may be treated with rest, liniment and massage, or cold packs. Closely examine the animal's recent history for some possible cause for which a countermeasure may be instituted.

Should the condition be chronic—the conformation of the horse himself may be the inciting cause—it is necessary to give permanent help. This is done by relieving some of the strain on the flexor tendons and suspensory ligament; raise the heel and shorten the toe. This way of trimming also helps by making the breakover easier, and it may be further improved with the use of a roller-motion or other "easy-action" shoe. Heel calks could be recommended in such a case.

Laminitis

Laminitis, commonly called "founder," in the horse is literally a circulatory derangement of the feet. The many causes, the chemistry, the definite diagnosis and the treatment of laminitis comprise a subject of depth; our need is to gain an understanding of the damage done in order to handle better the abnormal foot which laminitis often leaves in its wake.

Simply stated, the tiny vessels in the sensitive lamina become engorged. In a nonhoofed animal the feet would merely swell; in the unyielding casement of the hoof the swelling forces a separation of the sensitive lamina of the corium from their interlocking state with the horny lamina of the hoof wall. When this happens to the horse, the lamina are unable to regain their normal interdigitating position, and the separation is permanent. The coffin bone, whose shape corresponds to the inner contours of the hoof, is forced downward ("rotation").

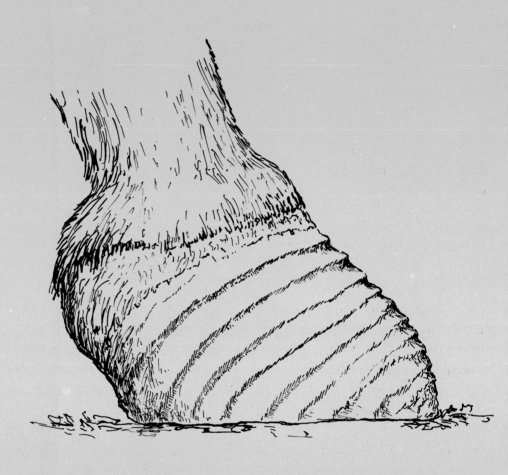

144   *Therapeutic Shoeing*

When the crisis is over and the animal is able to walk, he can usually be identified by the two-phase placement of the feet: heel-toe, heel-toe. This is one of the ways a foundered foot can look. Note the bulging toe, high heel and deep ridges.

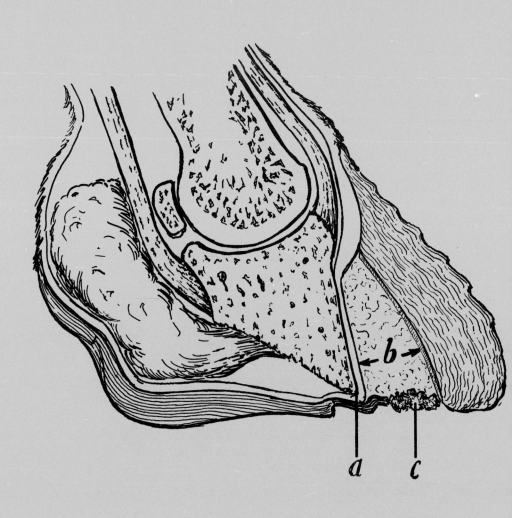

A sagittal section of the foot would show these abnormalities:

(a) Coffin bone rotated downward. Its angular free edge rests on the sole just anterior to the point of the frog.

(b) The coffin bone and corium are separated from the wall. By-products of inflammation occupy the intervening space.

(c) Cells at the distal ends of the sensitive lamina produce the horn of the white line. The imperfectly formed, overextended white line provides an ineffective seal against the entrance of filth and bacteria. When infection enters, the condition is called "seedy toe."

(d) During separation of sensitive lamina and wall, the sole also separates, at least partially, from the corium on the bottom of the coffin bone. When detectable, this is called "hollow sole" or "seedy sole."

(e) Due to chronic inflammation the wall grows abnormally fast, especially at the heel.

(f) The weight of the animal is normally transferred by way of the lamina to the wall of the hoof. Now this is not possible.

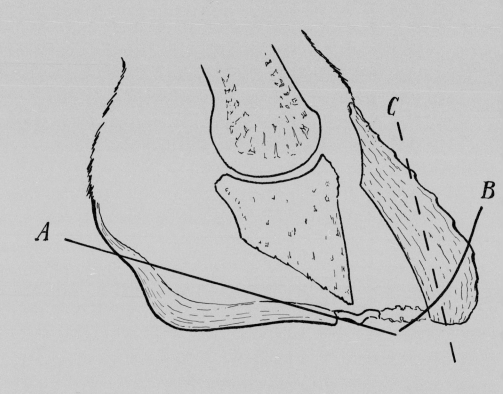

A horse so afflicted can never return to full soundness, but it is often possible to return him to usefulness through judicious trimming and shoeing.

(A) Trim off all the heel he can spare in order to bring the coffin bone more parallel with the ground.

(B) Shorten the toe to make the breakover as easy as possible.

(C) Various techniques for grooving the wall have been advocated. The purpose of grooving is to soften the rigidity of the wall, relieving internal pressure. It seems more appropriate to accomplish this end by thinning the wall with a rasp. Regular use of a hoof dressing is advised.

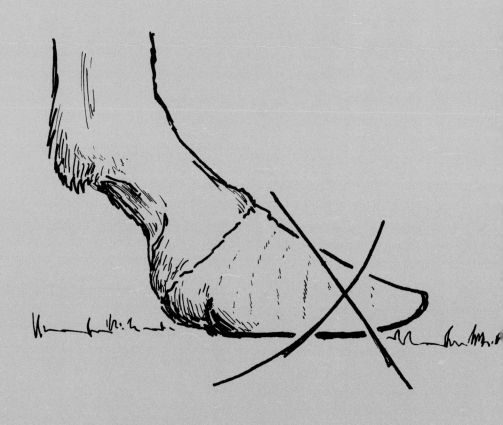

In the case of a horse whose toes grow out in sled-runner style, a surprising amount of toe can be removed without harm to the foot. Unconventional tools — a handsaw, for instance — may expedite the procedure. The wall of the toe may be rasped considerably to thin it and shape the hoof.

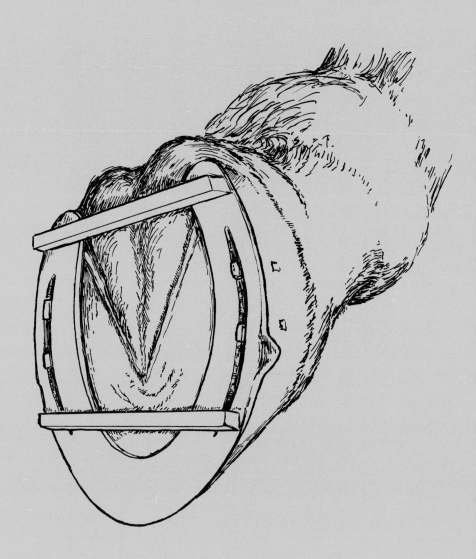

Therapeutic Shoeing

Upon observation of the improvement in performance and well-being of a foundered horse following reshaping of his feet, the decision may be reached to increase his usefulness with shoes. It would be convenient to be able to describe one good, simple shoe that would adequately serve the purpose, but no such shoe exists. Many good founder shoes have been developed, but no one shoe can fulfill the needs of all individuals. It is well, then, to determine the requirements of a founder shoe and to describe some of the more common practical measures that have been employed. In meeting the needs of a particular horse, the choice of shoes must rest on individual judgment.

Since the sole must bear more than its share of the weight, being unable to transfer it to the wall, some provision must be made for supporting the sole. The wall is not in good health, and so the fewest possible nails are used. No nails are driven in the toe. Some "easy-action" feature should be incorporated into the shoe.

This shoe has a wide web for support of the sole. Memphis calks are used; the toe calk is placed well back for easy breakover. Only four nails are driven, but they are supported by side clips.

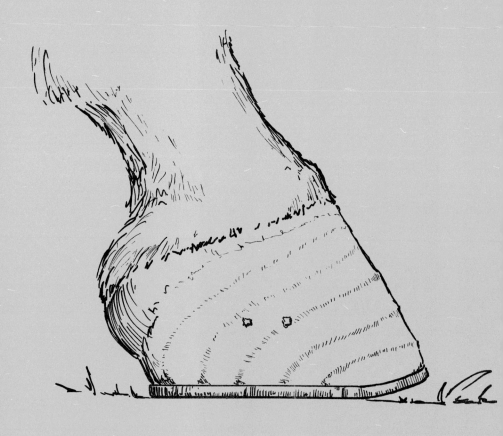

154   *Therapeutic Shoeing*

The roller-motion shoe is suitable.

Therapeutic Shoeing

A shoe with thinned toe and heel makes walking easier.

The foundered horse's way of landing on the heel sometimes causes the shoe to work forward. A heel clip may prevent this.

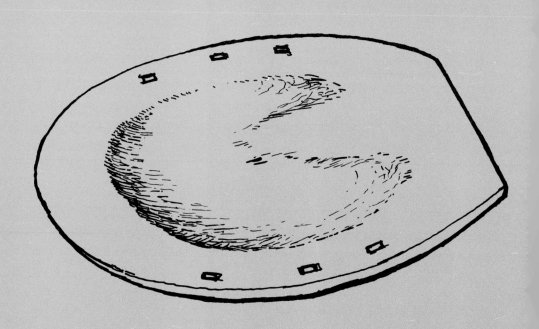

Leather pads between foot and shoe are often used. They are excellent for protection and support of the sole. Oakum and pine tar are packed between sole and leather, especially in the grooves. Cotton and hoof dressing make a satisfactory packing if they are more readily available.

Steel plates have been used in place of leather pads. When the sole is intact and the coffin bone does not protrude, they are perfectly satisfactory, and certainly provide firmer support. Plastic and rubber pads have also been used.

Shoes have been made of solid boiler plate, hollowed out on the anvil to fit the contour of the sole.

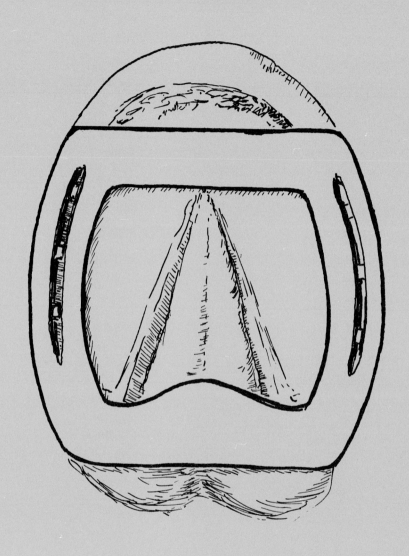

A limitation on the use of pads or plates may be the necessity to drain and treat seedy toe. In such a case, a shoe similar to this one may serve very well. The toe is accessible, easy breakover is afforded, and solid support for the coffin bone is provided. The bar, of course, increases frog pressure; a good finishing touch would be to rasp the wall at the toe very thin to allow dorsal dissipation of concussion.

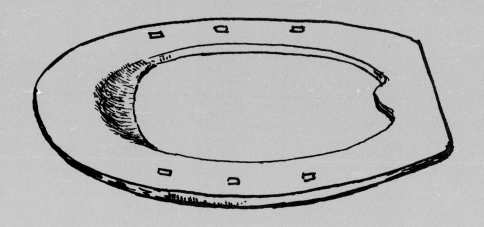

If seedy toe is not a problem, the toe can be full-fitted. If the coffin bone protrudes, it is an easy matter to hollow the wide toe to accommodate it.

Should seedy toe plus a sole weakened and tender from protrusion of the coffin bone present a dual problem, the same shoe can be varied by replacing the anterior bar with a strip of leather. The hoof wall may be recessed to make a notch for the leather.

The subject of laminitis is one without end. It can be researched quite thoroughly and yet provide opportunity for the application of ingenuity.

Chapter Nine

SHAPING
SHOES

The requirements attendant upon a good fit on the part of a horseshoe were described in Chapter Five. These requirements are best fulfilled by an expert farrier who shapes hot shoes individually to the feet of each horse entrusted to his expertise. The farrier's facility with forge and anvil is not easily or quickly acquired, and his equipment is expensive to assemble; unfortunately, his services are not available in all areas, forcing many of us into dependence on our own resources.

One alternative to this dilemma is to present a pattern of the horse's feet to a blacksmith. The quality of the pattern determines the outcome of this arrangement; so first prepare the feet for shoes. Trace the outlines of the left front and left hind feet on a board or cardboard, being especially accurate at the heel. Label the tracings.

Ready-shaped shoes may be purchased at a hardware store. The feet of horses are sufficiently uniform in shape to make this possible. Take a pattern of the feet with you in order to select the most suitable size; sizes range from 00, the smallest, to 8, which fits a very large draft horse. The front feet vary from the hind in size and shape and so, accordingly, do the shoes. Be certain to purchase a pair of each.

The store may stock only the standard factory "keg" shoe. These shoes also come in sizes and vary between those for the front and the hind feet. The heels of the shoe, which are long to allow for turning a calk, must be cut off at the proper length. This can be laboriously accomplished with a hacksaw, and the corners may be rounded off on a grindwheel. The nail crease is adequate for the nail heads, but the nail holes need to be enlarged with a pritchel, an operation to which cold steel does not respond.

Adapting preshaped shoes to feet is called "cold-fitting." For all practical purposes, the only changes that can be made in cold shoes are widening and narrowing. The former can be accomplished by prying the heels apart with the jaws or handles of a pincer or nipper. Narrowing is simply done with a hammer. In either case, the shoe usually becomes sprung and must be restored to the level condition by careful sighting and well-directed hammering or prying.

Ownership of the basic equipment of blacksmith and farrier, the forge and anvil, is impractical for most of us due to lack of skill in their use, the space required and the limited return for the expense involved. However, the subject is worthy of discussion for several reasons: the shaping of hot steel with a hammer is a fascinating pastime, sheer necessity may force this degree of self-reliance, or the convenience and versatility of such equipment on farm or ranch may justify its acquisition.

Before a forge is selected, observe one caution and consider several alternatives. Unless a source of high-grade blacksmith coal is assured, the purchase of a forge will prove to be unsatisfactory. A welder's cutting torch can heat steel to a malleable temperature and will ease the task of shortening heels on keg shoes. Gas appliances are available for the job; bottled gas forges are considered quite suitable by some traveling horseshoers, and some permanent shops have replaced their coal forges with natural gas as a source of heat.

If a coal forge is preferred, a choice must be made between hand- and electric-powered blower. The hand-operated blower is much more economical and mobile. It also lends itself to an improvised type of portable forge; a little pipe, fire clay and ingenuity can produce a very satisfactory firebed.

Anvils vary in size and quality; price will probably be the prime concern in selection. A 25-pound anvil may be quite adequate for one's needs, but a heavier anvil will give more satisfaction. A hammer blow on the face (working surface) of an anvil tells much about its quality: a resonant ring denotes quality steel; a dull thud, the reverse. Tap the base also in order to compare sounds. Many anvils are made of two grades of steel—high grade in the face, lower grade in the base. This is not mentioned to deter the purchase of such an anvil, but as a guide in comparison of values. Be certain that the anvil of choice has a square hole in the face near the heel (thin end).

Several basic tools must be accumulated—hammer and tongs, of course. If a coal fire is used, get a small shovel, a poker and tongs for removing clinkers. Choose a nail punch of high-quality steel for making and shaping the recesses for nail heads. A pritchel is vital. This is a punch, slimmer and more tapered than the nail punch, that is used for punching holes for the shanks of nails and opening up nail holes in keg shoes. It is also used for carrying hot shoes to horses for hot-fitting. Several tools with square shanks that fit the square hole in the anvil face will be available, but for the present one needs only the hardy. The hardy supplies a cutting edge for shortening the heels of keg shoes with the use of hammer rather than hacksaw or torch.

Once equipment and tools are assembled, and one stands ready to light the fire and pound steel, the inadequacy of the printed word becomes most evident. The proper grip on the hammer, where and how to hit the steel most effectively, and many other refinements of technique must come from instruction and experience. Observation and emulation are helpful; this is no hardship, for everyone enjoys watching a blacksmith at work. A few useful pointers, however, may be indicated.

The anvil is mounted on a firm, level stand, the horn to a right-handed operator's left. The face is at a level that first seems a little too low to be comfortable—approximately at the level of the hand with the arm held at the side.

A coal fire is easily started, and must be periodically cleared of clinkers. Clinkers form from any coal, but are more vexingly abundant when low-grade coal is used. Their presence causes slow, uneven heating of the steel.

A dull red color does not indicate that the steel is sufficiently hot. It will bend, but is not yet entirely under control. Attain a bright cherry-red color before applying the hammer. When overheated, the steel will be white-hot. In the hands of a blacksmith this is a proper heat for forge welding; to a tyro it simply means that the steel is being burned up and downgraded in quality. Characteristic sparking from the fire indicates when this critical temperature has been reached.

When fitting keg shoes, the first operation is to heat one heel, then either turn the calk or cut the heel to length. Then do the same with the other heel. Now heat the toe and turn a toeclip, if desired; then open the nail holes. Experience dictates how deep to drive the pritchel to fit a nail of a particular size. Shape the shoe, level it, turn the ground surface up, insert the pritchel in a nail hole and carry the shoe to the horse for a fitting. If extensive alterations are required, it is best to reheat the shoe. The tyro might well bypass the horse and fit the shoe to a traced pattern of the foot.

As familiarity with fire and tools grows, one may wish to purchase bar steel from which to fabricate shoes. Mastery of this process indicates an appreciable degree of advancement from the first awkward days of trembling under the weight of a horse and missing the anvil with the hammer. It gives one a considerable sense of satisfaction!

INDEX

Page numbers in italics indicate illustrations.

tendon of, *8*, 9
walls of, cracks of, *128*, 129
weights upon, *90, 91*
Forefoot, handling of, *18, 19, 20, 21, 22, 23*
Forge, firing of, 171
Forges, 169
tools used in conjunction with, 170
Forging, 57
correction of, 116
Founder, and laminitis, 143, *144, 145, 146,*
147
effect upon heel, *156, 157*

Gait, faults of, 114
improvement of, by corrective trimming, 45

Hammer, in shoeing, *78*
Handling the feet, 15–33
Heel, bulb of, 2
contracted, *132, 133, 134*
effect upon, of founder, *156, 157*
Heel cartilage, 7
Heel weight, and corrective shoeing, *94,*
95
Hindfoot, handling of, *24, 25, 26, 27, 28,*
29, 30, 31, 32, 33
Hipposandal, x
"Hollow sole," 147
Hoof, anatomy of, *2, 3, 4, 5, 6, 7, 8, 9, 10*
bar groove of, *4, 5*
blood in, 12
buttress of, *4, 5*
coronary groove of, *10*, 11
dressing of, 13
frog of, *5*
horny lamina of, *10*, 11
layers of, *3, 4*
parts of, *2, 3*
periople of, *10*, 11
pigmented layer of, *3, 4*
protective coating of, treatment of, 13
quick of, *10*, 11
sole of, *3, 4*
trimming of, 35–41
corrective, 43–68
wall of, *10*, 11
"white," *3*
Hoof knife, in shoeing, *78*

Hoof nippers, in shoeing, *78*
Horn, of hoof, moisture in, 13
protective coating of, treatment of, 13
Horny lamina, of hoof, *10*, 11
Horseshoe. See also *Shoe.*
handling forefoot to place, *18, 19, 20,*
21, 22, 23
handling hindfoot to place, *24, 25, 26,*
27, 28, 29, 30, 31, 32, 33
nails of, clinching of, *30*, 31
Horseshoeing, historical survey of, x
of Tennessee walking horses, 65

Interfering, correction of, 115

Knee-spring, *62, 63*
Knife, hoof, in shoeing, *78*

Lameness, after shoeing, 87
Laminitis, 143, *144, 145, 146,* 147
Leather pads, in therapeutic shoeing, *158,*
159

Memphis bar, *106, 107*
Muscles, digital flexor, and tendinitis, 142

Nail, aiming of, in shoeing, *80*, 81
Nail crease, of shoe, 73
Nail nippers, *78*
Nailing, of shoes. See *Shoes, nailing of.*
Nails, horseshoe, clinching of, *30*, 31
for shoes, 73, 74
Navicular bone, 7, *8, 138*
Navicular disease, *138*, 139, *140,* 141
Nippers, hoof, *78*

Ossification, of lateral cartilages, 137

Paddling, correction of, 115
Pads, leather, in therapeutic shoeing, *158,*
159
Pastern bone, *6*, 7
Periople, 2, *10*, 11
Physiology, of the foot, 12
Pincer, alligator, in shoeing, *84, 85*
pull-off, in shoeing, *78*

Quarter, *2*
Quick, of hoof, *10*, 11